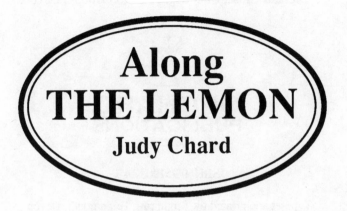

Along
THE LEMON
Judy Chard

THE LIFE STORY OF A DEVON RIVER

FROM HAYTOR TO NEWTON ABBOT

Best Wishes
Judy Chard

First published 1978
by Bossiney Books
ISBN 0 906456 02 9

This edition published 1993 by
Orchard Publications
2 Orchard Close, Chudleigh, Newton Abbot , Devon.

ORCHARD
PUBLICATIONS

ISBN 0 9519027 4 1

Typeset and printed by Teignprint, Teignmouth, Devon
in conjunction with BPCC Wheatons, Exeter, Devon.

Plate Acknowledgements

Cover photograph by Mike Frost
1, 2, 3 ,4, 5, 6, 7, 9, 10, 11, 12, 13, 14, 15, 17, 25 Ray Bishop
8 Mrs Woolner
16 Mrs Stoneman and Mr Holwill

1938 Floods - 18, 19, 20, 21 Vincent Bibbings - Gordon Babcock
22, 23, 24 Mid-Devon Advertiser

All 1979 flood pictures from the Mid-Devon Advertiser
taken by Rex Hitchcock, staff photographer, for the use of these
author and publisher would like to thank the Editor, Lance Samson.

BUCKINGHAM PALACE

3rd January, 1979

Dear Mrs Chard,

I am commanded by The Queen to thank
you for your charming present 'Along the Lemon'
which Her Majesty has read with great interest.
The chapter about Ogwell Mill is particularly
interesting in view of the fact that it is owned
by Lieutenant-Commander and Mrs. Holdsworth.

How lucky you are to live in that part
of the world!

Yours sincerely,

Robert Fellowes.

Mrs. J. Chard.

AUTHOR'S NOTE

Although I have, where possible, double checked all my facts, visited the places described, and followed the river from source to mouth, it is possible, as always when recounting history and anecdotes collected from people, that mistakes may occur, so I am quoting the Rev. D.M. Stirling from the preface to his book written in 1830 *A History of Newton Abbot and Newton Bushel*, in which he says 'Kindly impart, if you know better things. If not, then use those which the author brings.' Even then writers had their problems!

I would like too to show my appreciation to Ray Bishop for his beautiful photographs, and to thank all those people who responded so overwhelmingly to my request for information and photographs in their possession - too numerous to mention, but without them the book would not have been possible.

The maps I used were:
OS Newton Abbot Sheet SX 87/97 1:25000 2nd series.
OS Widecombe in the Moor Sheet SX 77 1:25000 1st series.

ALONG THE LEMON

BEGINNINGS

To stand on the actual spot where a river starts its life is a curious feeling - to watch the water bubbling up from the depths of the moor at one's feet as it starts its journey to the sea - although inevitably reminiscent of Tennyson's brook that went on forever - like man, it still has a beginning and an end, its yesterdays, todays and tomorrows are filled with the dramas, and tragedies, of life itself, which occur on or near its banks, all to become part of history.

One thing is certain, the River Lemon has been bearing its soft, peaty water to the Teign since the Bronze Age, for near the springs in Bagtor Mire where one tributary, the Sig, rises, there are hut circles where once an agricultural site stood by this source of water.

Some say the name Lemon comes from the Celtic word for elm, others that *Lemmon* is of Saxon origin taken from *Llammau* - stones, which, when associated with *Afon*, a river, means literally 'stones in a river to walk upon'. Before bridges were built in the neighbourhood, all the fords of the Lemon did have big stepping stones, some of which could still be seen crossing the river behind Wolborough Street until the year 1785, replaced by the Union Bridge in 1822 which is still in use today.

Unlike the Dart, the Lemon doesn't start in a remote part of the moor. In fact it is simple for anyone to find its 'beginnings' in a mire near the old Haytor main or No 1 Quarry, where work started in 1820 and Mr George Templer of Stover built his tramway to link Haytor with the coast. You can still see the foundations of the houses where the quarrymen lived. He also built a public house at Haytor Vale, with dwellings either side for the miners who, before then, had lived in cottages scattered about the moor.

At the feet of these workings the river starts. Not sluggish for long, soon it hurries with a kind of urgency over granite pebbles, its water bright and clear in the summer sunlight - seeming so harmless and peaceful, running under the road and past the burned-out ruin of the Moorland Hotel, a reminder of one of the many fires which have occurred on its banks.

Here, at its beginnings, controversy once raged, for water used to be taken from it to feed the leat or pot water, the sole supply for Ilsington village, and Dick Wills, parish historian of Narracombe, whose family have farmed there for fourteen generations, told me there were many accusations from the thirteenth century onwards that too much water was taken, thus depriving the manor mill, Bagtor, of its supply, whilst the leat was feeding the mills of Ilsington, Liverton and Pool.

'It seems,' he said 'that there was a trough at the source and from a hole in this the water ran through the fields to Ilsington. The villagers used to go and make the hole bigger so more water ran their way. This caused a certain amount of ill feeling!

But for a moment we come back to the present century. On the night of 6 March 1970, when the Bovey police and their 250 guests were enjoying their twenty-first annual ball, soon after midnight everyone was asked to file out of the ballroom into the courtyard, and as they went they saw smoke pouring from the air vents, and outside flames were leaping from the roof of the hotel.

The police tackled the fire with extinguishers until ten appliances arrived with sixty firemen, but all they could do was to stop the blaze from entirely destroying the hotel. A large section of the upper floor was wiped out and extensive damage caused to the ground floor. It was thought that the fire had started as the result of faulty wiring, but fortunately at least there were no casualties, four children who had been asleep upstairs being carried to safety. The following morning the police had to open up a special depot for people to pick up their coats at the police station in Newton Abbot, among them a silver mink. Much to everyone's relief the draw money and prizes had also been saved! It was the biggest hotel fire in the area for years, and now it is known as the Hotel with no Guests, for it has remained an empty shell ever since. All you can hear as you stand looking over the gate is the whistling of the wind through the glass-less windows. The owners did want to rebuild it on a bigger scale, but the plan was turned down by the Dartmoor National Park Committee. At the entrance is a board which states CLOSED UNTIL FURTHER NOTICE. Could it perhaps be forever?

Let us look now at something beautiful instead, for it is only fair to visit the Lemon's main tributary while we are on this part of the moor - the

6

River Sig which rises in Bagtor Mire under Rippon Tor - and here I quote from Crossing's Guide to Dartmoor where he says 'Risdon speaks of a noted place called Saddletor from the hills near which the Lomen or as we now call it, the Lemon - "fetcheth her fountain". The nearest stream to the tor is the Sig which rises on Bag Tor Down about 1/4 mile S of it . . . it falls into the Lemon (the springs of which are near Lud Gate) just below Sigford, and immediately after having received the waters of the Langworthy Brook.' All of which we shall be investigating in due course.

This particular stream, which becomes the River Sig, runs past Bagtor cottages and is typical of these moorland streams, deep set in ferns and bright flowers among the rocks as they chatter busily onwards, and it was here that Syd Wills, now living at St Budeaux, spent many happy hours of his childhood, and where he told me, 'It was an unwritten law to let the foxes drink before you collected the day's water supply from the brook.' He went on to tell me of the two ladies who once ran Bagtor House and the Barton as guesthouses and farm, their names Miss Blankiron and Miss Cross.

Memories of them too came from Miss Catherine Haines, now in her 80s and living at Bridford. She was a groom at Bagtor House in the 1920s. And here once again the tragedy of fire touched the Lemon's tributary, the Sig. Early one morning she got up at five to go cubbing and saw clouds of smoke coming from the neighbouring farm of Westabrook, an old thatched house standing near the banks of the river.

She rushed down to wake up the Retallick family, who lived there, and to help the oldest member of the family from his bed and into the barn for safety. Eventually the fire engine arrived, 'But,' she said, 'there was some problem over getting the pump started to take water from the stream, and I had to chase off to another farm for fuel.' Meanwhile Mr Retallick was concerned about his watch which, as was his habit, he had tied to the bedpost for the night. It was rescued - only to be stolen from him later. His son, Mr H. Retallick, now farms Bagtor Barton and he told me that recently when they were doing some repairs at Bagtor cottages they took down a partition and uncovered a small cubby hole like the ones from which tickets are sold at railway stations. 'My guess is that is where they paid the men who worked in Newtake and Crownley Mines,' he said 'and there are also the remains of a blacksmith's shop and blowing house on the common.'

He too remembered the two ladies from the Big House. 'Proper Victorians they were and a law unto themselves, everything revolved around Miss Blankiron. She always dressed in men's checked breeches with high boots and a bowler hat. She used to sit on an iron bench in the farm yard to give her orders . . . we had always to touch our caps to her of course.'

Miss Haines said 'Any quarrels among the staff were quelled by the contents of the pig bucket being thrown over the contestants. I know because it was usually my job to do it!'

It seems the two ladies didn't know much about farming, but they had managed to oust the original tenants from the Barton because they didn't like the smell of pigs. They managed to make life unbearable for them, and of course there was no security of tenure at that time.

'The old steam threshers used to come round in those days,' Mr Retallick said 'and Miss B put a barrel of cider in the field to keep the men happy . . . they got "happy" all right, and when the two ladies went to see how they were getting on with the job, they picked them up and set them on the pile of sacks calling Miss B "Mabel m'dear" . . . they got the sack all right, and the cider taken away.' He told me Miss Blankiron eventually died of a heart attack on the spot where the larder is now, adding slowly 'Like I said, she had to be different from everybody else.'

But Miss Haines remembered the Big House - Bagtor - being in a rather run-down state. The bedroom she slept in, with her terrier for company, was noisy with rats at night. She took up the floorboards and with a poker - and the help of the dog - killed twelve of the rats in one night. Today it is a very different proposition having been beautifully restored and with an American lady called Mrs Perrin living there. The rear portion of the house is Elizabethan, the front part being built in Queen Anne style, and Dick Wills told me, 'I have some accounts of it in 1770 in which it is spoken of as a "modern house", but we must remember that in Devon they were about fifty years behind in their styles - in other words the architecture of Queen Anne, current in London during her reign, was copied some fifty years later down here!

The house has an interesting history for John Ford, the Elizabethan dramatist and poet, lived there, having been baptised at Ilsington Church on 12 April 1586 according to the parish register. He was perhaps most famous for an imaginative and dramatic study of incest between brother

1. Beginnings - source of River Lemon by Haytor Quarries

2. Beginnings - the Sig under Ripon Tor

3. The Moorland Hotel after the fire.

4. The river's first job - Bagtor Mill

5. Bagtor House

6. The river grows up. Sigford where 3 streams meet.

and sister in *'Tis Pity she's a Whore*, and the chronical play *Perkin Warbeck*. Most of his life was spent in London, but it is said he returned to Bagtor House to die, although there is no proof of it and no record of his burial in the register - another mystery that haunts this river.

In the latter part of the seventeenth century Sir Henry Ford, twice Secretary of State for Ireland, lived there during Charles II's reign, so in spite of its isolation it saw much of contemporary life.

Miss Haines left the big house in the summer and went to the cottages on the moor: 'My bedroom window looked over Bagtor Mire to Rippon Tor one way, and the other over Pinchaford and down to the Teign and the estuary.' Thankfully this spot is still unspoilt with the wild bleakness of the tors in contrast to the soft beauty of Bagtor Wood with its beeches and avenue leading to the farm, the Sig still sparkling and chattering alongside and, like all rivers, changing constantly over the course of the day on its travels.

We are inclined to forget that if it wasn't for the streams and rivers on Dartmoor - fourteen at least - the whole history of the county would have been different. They were responsible for most of the industry at one time, the oldest being tin streaming and the wool trade of both the Middle Ages and later, which would have been impossible without their freely-given energy. There would have been no wool merchants, no towns with busy looms, no spinning wheels in the villages, no beautiful churches, no noise and clatter of the fulling mills on the banks of streams, no cloth markets in the towns and cities, and no pack horses with their loads travelling on inexorably to the ports. The nuns and monks of England and other European countries would not have had their warm habits of Devon Kersey to wear - all this arising from the peaty bogs and mires of Dartmoor - and even our modest little river played an important part in this history, becoming truly industrious as it grew from a stream to a river, having to earn its living, learning to grow up quickly and go to work.

The first water wheel it turned was that of Bagtor, the mill being mentioned in the Ilsington Church Terrier of 1727 when the Vicar of that parish, the Rev. Philip Nanson, claimed title on all sorts of corn and grain ground there, and at 'Ingsden, Levaton and Pool Mills', which were also water mills in the parish of Ilsington.

Bagtor used to belong to Mr Retallick, but he sold it to the present owners who rebuilt it. The old wheel dated 1875 exists, but sadly there is now no machinery although the leat still runs and a beautiful water garden surrounds the building beneath the cool shade of many trees. In the grounds there is a small cottage known as Millcombe where the parlour maid at Bagtor House, Carrie Harvey, once lived with her husband. Miss Haines used to exercise her horses in these woods when the weather was too rough on the moor 'and many a good cup of hot cocoa Carrie made for me . . . '

Now the Lemon runs on, leaving the first mill behind, having a respite as it tumbles through Smith's wood.

SMITH'S WOOD TO SIGFORD

You can enter Smith's wood either from Bagtor Mill end, or from Sigford itself where a lane leads up to Smith's Wood cottage, now called Kate's cottage. This was most likely once a miner's cottage standing in a typical Devon wood with a mixture of beech, oak and hazel, carpeted with moss and, in their season, rich with the colour of bluebells, pink campion and the deeper crimson of foxgloves, the lower branches of the trees entwined with dog roses and sweet smelling honeysuckle, a paradise of peace and beauty, and always the sound of running water like background music . . .

Just under a mile from the road stands the cottage. Mr Retallick had warned me there had been changes, the trees cut down, the ground levelled, and a new house built, but it still came as something of a shock to see the present building with its wooden shutters, a new cesspool and storage tanks, and the 'up and over' metal door to the garage. Perhaps most incongruous of all amidst this sylvan peace, a yellow alarm bell marked Securicor shining garishly on the wall. It seems the lane had been dug up so the alarm cable might be laid and taken to the police station in Ashburton. It all seemed a little larger than life - as one of the locals said, she couldn't remember a crime of any sort taking place in the area! Such perhaps is progress.

In the village of Sigford itself the Lemon really becomes a fully grown river, for it is joined by its two companions - the River Sig of which I have already written, itself swollen now by Langworthy brook meeting it under an arch from where the two of them flow into the Lemon a few yards further on.

16

The Langworthy Brook has been the cause of quite a bit of controversy in the past and I myself have seen water the colour of tomato soup run past our house! This it seems is due to 'they arsenic mines' at Owlacombe. These were worked up until the 1920s for arsenic and tin, and the streams which run down into the brook carry ochre. Thus when the springs rise and the mines flood, all this colours the water which eventually reaches the Lemon.

In spite of the consternation, it apparently is harmless to man and beast.

On the opposite side of the road are the Owlacombe Beams, very old workings which some people say could go back to Roman times. They are medieval at least, open cast, and were once worked by hand.

At the cross roads in the village a mill stood for grinding corn, but in 1710 disaster struck the family who lived there, wiping out seven children and the mother, the father being the only survivor. The Nosworthys were the millers thus affected, Dick Wills' ancestors, and he said, 'It may have been the plague or small pox, we don't know, but by some miracle the father escaped, he returned to Manaton and eventually married again.'

I looked for the site but could only find the barns and outhouses; it is still called The Mill and the leat can be seen.

Risdon in his book, where he alludes to the moor as 'The mother of many rivers' remarks that 'in character they are similar, and yet each I think has a peculiar beauty of its own as it comes from some boggy hollow or swampy tableland and at first their course is silent and sluggish, but not for long as other brooks come to augment their volume and they become streams hurrying over a bed of granite pebbles, through border valleys among trees that clothe their banks. Their water is bright and clear although near the source they may well be the colour of the bog in which they rise due to the bed of the stream being coated with a deposit washed down from the mire in which it rises, this is called argillaceous loam, reddish in colour which the bog rests on.'

This is a perfect description of the Lemon now, where down the lane to the left, the three rivers meet, and having done its job of work at two mills, it curls and meanders on through Goodstone woods, a beautiful rural setting not unlike Smith's Wood. I walked up through the trees to Hooks Cottage, I suppose again either a miner or keeper's home, now washed pink, set among tulips and daffodils out in all their glory on the spring day I saw it, and somehow reminiscent of Hans Anderson. Just before you reach its gate the footpath turns off to the right, a notice telling you the footbridge is not to be used for horses who must brave the ford. From here you can walk the country mile back to Sigford along the river bank, through woodland and open meadow, the river curving like a snake, or in the other direction, to Bickington where you now hear the ceaseless roar of the traffic on the A38 dual carriageway, our first taste of modern civilisation. Behind you, apart from the 'pink pink' of the chaffinches, the song of the blackbird and the call of the cuckoo, all is still peace and tranquillity.

BICKINGTON. BY THE OLD MILL STREAM...

Apart from the town of Newton Abbot itself where in the olden days the Lemon was literally part of its lifeblood, possibly this small and rather scattered village had more work for the river than anywhere else in the heyday of the watermill.

Nellie Dean and her beau may have dreamed by the old mill stream, but Devonians, who have earned their bread for hundreds of years through the mills and their streams and leats, certainly didn't have much time to do so. Many of the early mills in Devon were quite small and could be worked by one or two members of the family, parish apprentices, and labourers, the occupier devoting the rest of his time to farming.

There are not very many Devon mills actually recorded in Domesday book, only about 94 in contrast to 368 in Somerset, and most of them are located east of the Exe, possibly because the watermill was a technical improvement which had advanced from the east and had not yet ousted the hand mill from most of the rest of Devon, but it is also possible that the mills listed in Domesday may not have been comprehensive. The mill on the manor would be mentioned because it had become usual for the lord to let or farm out his monopoly mill rights to a miller, and the rental therefore was part of his wealth, and of course all farmers in the respective manors had to take their corn to the manor mills to be ground so that the lord might take his due.

Both wind and water power have been used extensively to drive mills in Devon, but the water wheels, with which we are concerned, in our River Lemon, were of two types - overshot, where the water was carried to the

18

top of the wheel by a launder driving it from above, and the undershot driven by the force of the water thrusting against the lower vanes. Other variations were pitchback and high or low breasted.

The most interesting and important function of rivers since man first came to this earth, was the turning of water wheels to make power, above all, as we have seen, for the mills which dotted the banks of rivers. As this is not an academic study, I do not intend to go into the technical details of these, sufficient to say that to get the surface speed from slow moving shafts, there had to be giant stones of varying textures - and please remember to use the proper terms of reference in this connection! You BRUISE oats, CRUSH barley and GRIND wheat!

Returning to the mills in which we are interested - Bickington was the first the Lemon reached in the village. The building still stands beside a dry leat below the built-up flyover for the new road. Here at one time flock was made which was used for the stuffing of horses' collars, the seats of furniture and so on. It was made from old rags which were torn up and processed, in this case the wheel drove what is called a devil or spiked mill for tearing the rags before manufacture.

Mr Gordon Johns, who went to live at Bickington in 1899, told me: 'My grandfather worked the mill, then my father, and then my father and I. It was known as The Mills, Bickington. We made flock for mattresses and wool for horses' saddles, and collars. The cylinder of the devil machine had about five to six hundred very sharp steel spikes set in apple wood and it travelled at 500 revs per minute. The best saddler's wool was made from Dutch carpets which came from Holland in bales of about five hundredweights. There was a large washing machine and a carding machine with several rollers and thousands of very fine teeth on them. The wool from this machine was made chiefly for saddlers, the best in the Mill. There was a large dust extracting machine, the dust being sold to the village people for their gardens at 2s 6d a cwt, a splendid manure for all green vegetables. The Mill was a four storey building, built of limestone, with walls about two feet thick. The water wheel was some fifteen feet diameter and about four feet wide. It was between two and three hundred years old and well built. We regulated the flow of water at a weir in the River Lemon close to Yeo Farm.'

The next mill was called Lemonford. This once stood on the old part of the Ashburton to Newton Abbot road, but it was totally destroyed by fire and only the bare bones of foundations remain among trees and brambles, although the old leat can still be seen in the fields, running in a loop and back into the river.

Mr Tom Daw of Kingkerswell told me the story of how it was burnt down in 1881 when his grandfather was miller. The circumstances can only be described as bizarre. The launder, or wooden trough, which carried the water down over the wheel and inside the building, had a lever controlled by a piece of cord to prevent the water running over the wheel when it was not required to turn. On this particular night the rats chewed through this cord, thus releasing the lever. The water started to run down the launder and turned the wheel which started the millstones to grind . . . as there was no corn between their surfaces, they became red hot and set the mill alight. Before help could come, it had burned to the ground.

'Often a mill had to work all through the night,' Mr Daw said, 'otherwise we couldn't cope with all the work, and sometimes we had to get up because we heard the wheel running too fast, and then at other times during a drought, we could only work for two or three hours. The 3ft 6in stones ground about a hundredweight an hour and there were times when we had to pinch more water from the river by putting stones down to drive it to our own particular leat!' Shades of those thirteenth century water thieves!

I asked him what killed the grain mills and he said, 'Like so many things - progress, if you like to call it that! The coming of the combine. In the old days when the thresher had to go all round the parish the grain was dry . . . now we had to buy expensive machinery to dry it, put in hammers going at speed and not choking, so in a very short time the mills disappeared. I can remember forty-five at least at one time in the Ashburton area alone . . . they seemed to go almost over night.'

And so they may have done, but the Lemon still flowed on, its work load lessened. It flowed next past the old pub now called the Dartmoor Halfway, its name coming from the fact that it stands half way between the old stannary town of Ashburton and Newton Abbot. It is possible that before the seventeenth century farm cottages with small holdings stood there, but when it became a pub it was visited by the travelling brewer from Newton Abbot and he added the steps on the side in the eighteenth century. Actually the rough stone and cob of the original is hard to date and there is no mention in the county records of the building, but I did find its position on an 1813 map in the county record office - not actually named as such.

Mr Jimmy Young of Crediton, an expert on old inns, told me it was most likely used as a drovers' stop on the route from the moor to Newton Abbot market, and Mr Brian Huggins, the landlord, said there are still signs of the old dormitory where they slept, above the present day bar.

It was too a 'change house' for the horses when the small coach business developed on the main Plymouth to Exeter route from Newton Abbot. These horses were also available for private carriages and this brought prosperity to the inn which was eventually taken over by the Heavitree Brewery.

Before we leave Bickington there are two local people to visit. Mrs Waterman, who now lives at Halshanger Cross, was born and lived as a small child in Goodwill Cottage near the banks of the river in the village. 'My brother and I often went fishing in the Lemon, and once he came home with an eel wrapped round the handlebars of his bike. He carefully unravelled it and dragged the hook out of its mouth, putting it in the pond as company for the goldfish! But in the morning it had gone. Had it been stolen by birds or had its relatives collected it we wondered . . . or perhaps the call of the wild attracted it back to its mating ground.' She went on to tell me that often they waded up stream. 'Parts of the river were very deep, above our thighs. We pulled out all sorts of rubbish, but no fish. The river had a peculiar smell of its own, rather like dead fish, or how I thought they would smell, mixed up with the stagnant odour of cow dung and urine!'

I feel certain the old river had watched generation after generation of small children doing exactly the same - long may they continue to do so.

But without doubt our best well known local character is Owen Caunter, at the moment preparing his own book of stories in dialect, at which he is a past master. He has appeared on television and radio many times for although he is mainly a farmer, he is also an expert on the ancient and genuine method of cider making, which he has often demonstrated in public, and a gifted thatcher and corn dolly maker.

He lives at Bonemill, once called Chipley Mill, and here they made the serge or Kersey for which Devon was so famous. The mill employed 150 people and he showed me the crooks driven into the beams where the old machines had stood. At the end of his garden runs the river, and the weir which controlled the leat for the next mill downstream - Ingsdon - at one time belonging to Miller Thorne. Here, although the house and buildings still stand beside the leat, which runs full and free, and the high lift on the building which raised the sacks of corn can be seen, unfortunately the very day before a preservation order was due to be put on the wheel itself, it was removed.

The river is now reinforced by the Kester Brook which joins it at the foot of Prairie field, belonging to my neighbour, Lionel Stanbury, who farms along the banks of the river for more than a mile.

Owen told me the Kester rises from many springs - from Hole and Burne Combe and Farlacombe, through Washing Pool where it is said the devil used to wash his shirt out at midnight, then go back up the lane to an old pollard oak where he hung it to dry near Hole Farm.

But it is time for us to follow the river as it now hurries on down to its next job of work . . .

HOLBEAM AND OGWELL MILL

Whether these two mills are really the most interesting historically one cannot be certain, but we do have more details of their past than of the others. In the field opposite our house is the weir which controls the leat to Holbeam, or Hobbim as it appeared, as a flour mill, in William the Conqueror's Domesday book, to be joined by yet another stream, on some maps described as the Blackford Brook, by others as Barham.

As to the mill, I can do no better than quote from the *Torquay Times* dated Christmas Day 1935, kindly lent to me by Mr B. Loder: 'Tucked away down a tiny Devon lane on the banks of a delightful little river, the Lemon, just above the bridge where the river and woodlands of Bradley manor meet, two and a half miles from Newton Abbot, stands Holbeam Mill. This ancient building, old enough to be mentioned in Domesday book, at a casual glance appears to be just an ordinary smithy. In those far off Saxon days it was a flour mill. About 200 years ago it was converted and machinery installed to produce knives and fish hooks for the Newfoundland cod fish industry. About 80 years later it was taken over by a family of blacksmiths who added tilt hammers to its outfit and commenced the manufacture of agricultural edge tools, scythes, bill hooks, mattocks and suchlike implements. This business has survived against the competition of mass production and is still being carried on by members of the same family. These blacksmith craftsmen in steel are working today

22

7. Owen Caunter on Chipley Bridge - rebuilt after 1938 flood.

8. Old Ogwell Mill.

9. New Ogwell Mill.

10. "The Drovers Return"!

with the same primitive machinery and the same time honoured methods, forging and tempering on open fires, good honest steel tools which they sell at Newton Abbot every market day. Long may they flourish.'

Sadly they only 'flourished' until 1943, when the Loder family, as they were called, had to give up owing to ill health after three generations of working the mill. But many of their beautifully fashioned tools, bearing their name, are still cherished in Devon farmhouses.

In those days there were two wheels, one to drive the hammers which beat out the material or metal, and another for blowing the fire to heat it.

As for the knives and fish hooks made for the fishing industry in earlier days, these too had been of such fine workmanship that a Sheffield mill had tried to imitate and sell its own wares under the mark 'Stockman - Warranted'. Mr Stockman, who then owned Holbeam, was so angry he sued the swindlers for damages; and obtained £600 from them - a large sum in those days I suppose.

Actually Holbeam was one of the last hammer mills to survive in England, and when it was finally abandoned, a small army of men arrived from London to take down the machinery, which they did with infinite care, numbering all the parts so it could be set up in the South Kensington Science Museum, where it can now be seen.

Today it is difficult to imagine, as you stand in the beautifully furnished hall of the mill, with one of the graceful Loder billhooks above the fireplace, that the building once resounded with all the noise of the machinery, where heavy hammers beat out tools and a furnace blazed.

Mr Loder told me that his family, which he had traced back for 300 years, had always been interested in tool making - but his clearest memory as a child was when they cleaned out the leat once a year and then fished for trout in the clear water. 'I remember too during the war, when the Germans had bombed Newton Abbot station, the plane came right out round where we were standing in the paddock by the mill. We thought it was going to land, but the pilot just waved to us and flew off.'

When I asked him why he thought Loder tools were so highly prized, he said 'Nowadays a hook or similar tool is made only of steel. We made them of iron which would literally wear forever. The iron was opened up and a layer of steel for the actual cutting edge welded in so you got an even flow as you cut.'

The present owners of the mill are Lt Commander John Holdsworth,

Gentleman Usher to the Queen, and his wife. Recently he was High Sheriff of Devon and to celebrate his appointment he held a garden party in the gardens of the mill among a riot of summer flowers, the sound of the river on one side, and on the other the rhythmic dripping of the leat on the remaining mill wheel. This garden, fashioned over the years with love and dedication, was a perfect setting for the marquee and the silver band, all of which must have confused the mallard who nests each year at the side of the leat, and the dipper who roosts above the front door, sometimes flying round the dining room, possibly checking the guest list!

The Holdsworth family can trace their ancestors to John de Haldeworth in 1275, the name acquiring its present form in 1541, the Rev. Robert Holdsworth, vicar of Modbury being the first of the name encountered in Devon. But to prove once more that truth is stranger than fiction, during the reign of the first Elizabeth one of her sheriffs of Devon was Richard Reynell who lived in the parish of Ogwell - as does John Holdsworth in the reign of the second Elizabeth!

The site of the last mill in a rural setting is Ogwell, but sadly nothing of the original seventeenth century house with its Dutch gable remains. There is only a small modern bungalow complete with TV mast, a few stones, and an old arch to show where the original building stood. But I am indebted to Mr H. Webber of Rose Cottage, Ogwell, whose family have lived in the village for over a hundred years, for some further details of this mill.

'I remember a family called Loder living there as flour millers - I went to school with the children - but just before 1909 when the manor and parish was sold up by Robert Scratton, the family went to America and I've heard nothing of them since. But when I was working on the road to the mill just before the last war, I remember a lorry coming and collecting up a big load of scrap iron from the ruins of the wheel and so on. I heard it was sold to Germany for munitions so maybe it was thrown back at us as bombs!'

He lent me a booklet dated 6 October 1898 on the History of Ogwell in which the following description of the mill is given. 'On the banks of the River Lemon and near the boundary line of the parish is situated Ogwell Mill in the Bradley Woods, of great antiquity and originally a monastery. The old mill is nestled amid the most lovely scenery in South Devon and is a frequent resort during the summer months of tourists from all parts. In the vicinity are several lofty hills from which fine views can be obtained.

28

The celebrated mass of marble full of madrepore is situated in the limestone chain on this property in the Vale of Ogwell near Chercombe Bridge, Westhill. The marble is composed of secondary limestone and forms a part of the grand chain which intersects the district. In a part of this hill near White Rock a splendid mass of stone containing madrepore corals, eucrinites and other animal remains was discovered many years ago by Mr Sharland of Torquay.'

All of which bears out the memories of Mrs Pope who lived there as a child and remembers that in the Victorian period people used to take what were known as feather fossils from the river and polish them to make up into brooches much in fashion then. But before the first world war the main attraction of the mill was its picturesque appearance and people came from miles around to paint and photograph it. You could also get a first class cream tea, but this stopped during the years of the war. Later the owner decided to open it again, and all was prepared, when an inspection was made by the Council to make sure the premises were suitable for public use. They were not, in fact they were declared dangerous and unsafe and indeed shortly after, during a severe storm, part of the house did collapse, the gable end surviving only for a short time until that too became a ruin.

Mrs Woolner of Bradley has a very interesting theory about this mill. 'Probably the Ogwell mill mentioned in Domesday is not the one on this particular site for this mill was worked by a leat which still runs, and the development of these was much later, during the seventeenth century. Prior to that a mill had direct use of the river,' and to emphasise her point she told me that lately she had found a pile of enormous stones lower down river. 'I am fairly certain this is the site of the original mill and that this almost cyclopian masonry, which at first sight appears to be a tumble of natural rock, is in actual fact the remains of the old mill pond which they made before leats to act as a dam, and then carried the water over the wheel in a launder, or put them directly into the river and undershot, in other words the water pushed the wheel from below, which was really most uneconomic. This site as such is emphasised by the fact that an old lane goes up the other side from these rocks towards the village, but there is no corresponding lane this side, the manorial mills for this bank all being down in Newton Abbot.' An interesting and entirely feasible theory.

A RIVER AT MY GARDEN'S END

Just before we go on to Bradley House and then become urbanised, let me quote Jonathan Swift who had always wanted 'A river at my garden's end, a Terrace walk and half a rood of land set out to plant a wood.' Well the first I have, over the last I have had to compromise by planting as many trees in my small plot as possible. I fear it is certainly not a wood. But I do know what it must be like to live in a mill for we can hear the river twenty four hours of the day and judge its temper by the sound.

When we first came to live here nearly three decades ago, there were otters, particularly in the area of the weir which, like many others, stored water for the mill a quarter of a mile down river. Now, with these mills gone, many of the weirs have fallen into disrepair and the deep pools have vanished. When we had the severe drought I thought if only the weirs could be repaired we should have a plentiful supply of water for a dry summer, and also encourage the return of the otters and trout. I am thankful to say otter hunting no longer takes place, the only pity that it has ceased being the fact that they did kill some of the mink which have lately bedevilled the river. The redoubtable centenarian Major Mott hunted the hounds in the days I remember. At one time they were kept at Glazebrook in South Brent under the master Major Green, and were said to be the oldest pack in Devon, possibly in England, foxes also being hunted by the same pack called the Dartmoor.

Mr Retallick told me he had not seen an otter for many years: 'We used to have one come up from Westabrook under the bridge. You could tell where he'd been because there were a few rocks in the middle of the river all clean with no moss where he'd crawled over them. When I was twelve I remember a trapper telling me of an otter travelling from this brook to Langworthy across the fields, going from stream to stream only when it was a heavy dew on the grass . . . they travel up river like herons.'

And a pair of these nest every year near our house. Often I have seen five or six in a field, hunched round in a semicricle by the river like aged directors at a board meeting. Then one will give a kind of half hearted hop, subside again, and gradually, one by one, they take off, an ungainly business usually accompanied by a stream of white bird lime! But once airborne they have a graceful, effortless flight, gliding upwards on warm thermals, their wings stiffly outstretched, then turning upstream, fly on, showing the weather coming from the moor is mild and calm, otherwise they would stay in a low, sheltered pasture near where the river slowly winds. Mr Retallick has herons too: 'They stand on one leg watching till my neighbour's car leaves the mill below, then they fly down and take the fish from the ornamental pond! I bet he wonders where they've gone! You can see those birds working it all out.'

Sadly now I never see kingfishers which used to dart all summer over the river like bright jewels, and Mr Bath, local historian and keen fisherman, told me 'Once when I was fishing I saw a hole in the bank opposite, out came a kingfisher. It flew off, returning later making a peculiar kind of twittering noise. The youngsters stuck their heads out of the hole, then came out and perched on a root and the parent fed them with tiny fish. I didn't care if I didn't catch anything myself that day - just to see that was enough.'

And talking of fish - a newspaper cutting of July 1972 states that 1500 fish were caught in the River Lemon above Newton Abbot according to the Devon River Authority's annual report. The fish included five adult migratory trout, 428 salmon parr and 1035 brown trout, all of which were later returned to the river below Newton Abbot.

All of which reminded me of the old couplet about fish in Devon 'The Teign for salmon, the Dart for peel, Ford leat for trout and the Lemon for eel!' This last being borne out by Mr Cowell of Newton Abbot, who told me as a boy when he went to visit his grandfather at Wolborough House for holidays, during May and June he would go down the garden to where the river ran and come back with a bucketful of elvers. Mostly in our part of the river there are small brown trout. In the spring a wet fly is best to use for when the river is high the water is rapid and boisterous and only here and there will a dry fly have much chance of floating for more than a second or two. Mill leats provide a marvellous sport in the dog days of summer when the usual water courses are shrunk with drought. I once caught a 14oz trout with a blue bottle - very unsporting to the purist I suspect! I also caught a swallow as it swooped through the air to tease the dogs, as I was casting. Fortunately I managed to get the barb out of its beak and it flew off, apparently unharmed.

We have a badger sett, whose whereabouts I shall not reveal for obvious reasons. I have no doubt that successive generations have lived there long

31

before man came to gas them, and it is a tribute to their ingenuity that they have survived being hunted by dogs, shot at, trapped, baited and now gassed. Normally they are creatures of the night, but if you are lucky enough to see one jogging along like a belated reveller, they do look much like small bears. I have watched them come down to the Lemon to drink, and marvelled, looking at their setts, at the amount of stones, rock and shale they can shift. I am delighted it is at least illegal to dig or trap them. As long ago as 1850 the actual so called sport of badger baiting was prohibited, I'm sorry to say this was very much practised before in Devon.

Foxes too abound. One hot summer afternoon I was lucky enough to see five cubs playing like kittens in the wood. I froze where I stood and although they looked straight at me, for nearly an hour they went on gambolling while I stayed entranced, cramped, but determined not to move. Later I saw their mother slip down the river bank and bathe in the water, rolling over, splashing and snapping at the spray just like a dog.

Hares are plentiful. I watch them in March, dancing, boxing and carrying on in the approved mad fashion, then sobering up, combing their ears to make them shine like the girls brush their hair. Sometimes, if I see one before he sees me, I walk towards him just for the delight in watching him suddenly crouch down flat so that it almost impossible to see him. Perhaps as I pass he will stay where he is, not because he is confident I won't hurt him, but simply because hares get to know that often to stay completely still is safer than running.

Each year a pair of tame mallards, escaped from some park I suppose, build their nest in the river bank below the paddock, the male all swank and green sheen comes up the yard when he hears the rattle of the hens' bucket. The female is a very sorry exponent of women's lib. following demurely behind, quietly waiting her turn, never pushing, and each year I am again amazed at the way in which those tiny balls of black fluff are launched on the water in a kind of hassle of hysteria, Ma cruising along behind, or in front, as the occasion demands, keeping up a running commentary of quacks like a T.V. announcer at the boat race, showing off so you can almost see the smile on her beak.

Inevitably all rivers must have bridges to carry the roads or lanes, and ours is no exception. This particular one was once a beautiful sight, a typical hump back pack horse bridge, widened for carriages on their way to Torbryan no doubt, but still good to look at. Then it was knocked down by the constant passing of a four wheeled 24 ton lorry, the blocks of granite pluging into the stream below. I suppose eventually it will be replaced, possibly by some horror of breeze blocks and cement, although I have done all I could with preservationists and so on, saying in despair 'God Save our Gracious Bridge'. Even the hedges and banks are being bulldozed, destroying this beautiful landscape which was probably created as far back as 1150 with its lanes leading down to lonely farms, the double hedgerows now only showing where possibly the original pack horse tracks ran - and if in your piece of hedge you can count ten different species of plant, then it has probably stood there for a thousand years

Our stretch of river has given us moments of panic too, apart from when it rises with rapidity, making me dash upstairs with any portable valuables, sure this time it will not 'stay 'way from my door!' But the worst fright we had was when I espied a surveyor with rods, poles, etc., on the banks and discovered a reservoir site was threatened. I fought a long and tedious battle, I think with hindsight, unnecessarily for in all probability the rock formation in Bradley woods would not have been suitable for the proposed dam, so at the moment the valley and woods remain peaceful and brimming over with interest and history.

BRADLEY WOODS

Going in this end from Chercombe bridge through the kissing gate by the half timbered house, I am reminded of the fact that once two cottages stood here, in which Mr Baker of Newton Abbot told me his gran lived. She too provided cream teas for the weary traveller, and bottles of Ross's lemonade. She had a tame otter that came into the kitchen for food, but often the cottages were flooded and her first thought when this happened was to move her pig to higher ground in the wood where she tied it to a tree, for in those days most cottagers would not have existed but for their pig so his safety was almost as important as that of the family itself!

It is possible the name Chercombe has arisen from the fact that there are many wild cherry trees in the valley and an old map shows an extensive cherry garden between the leat and river further down, but perhaps the point of greatest interest here is the first, and as far as I know,only, ghost story connected with the Lemon.

Two ladies in this house have vouched for the fact that they have heard, if not seen, a galloping horse on the road close by, always at night and usually at a time of storm - the galloping ceasing just as suddenly as it started. This has happened too many times and to people of such commonsense that it cannot be discounted. What is even more strange is that it wasn't until after they had heard this that they found out it ties up with a ghost at the Manor House standing at the other end of the woods, for in about 1750 the western wing, consisting of the stables, was demolished. Two hundred years later an elderly visitor repeated to the owner that her grandmother who had been in service in the house, told her these stables had been so badly haunted they had been allowed to fall into ruin. The ghost was that of a young man on horseback, the son of the house who had been killed in a riding accident. At the time his horse, in the flesh, had returned riderless to the stables. Now its shadow still does . . .

Back to the tangible - here abouts the bank of the river leads up to some high crags known as the pulpit or white rock which is of great interest to geologists as the local limestone, as stated earlier, is rich in fossils, and the many lime kilns in the area show that the stone was widely quarried here and burnt locally. The white rock itself is described by the Rev. Stirling in his book on Newton Abbot, written in 1830, thus - 'The celebrated white rock . . . is a piece of rude masonry, greatly assisted by the hand of nature, projecting in a frightful attitude from an angular point of the rock over the deep dell.' And as we walk on through the woods beside the river I can do no better than quote from another ancient book on Newton Abbot written by Rhodes. 'Bradley Woods - of premier importance . . . it is difficult if not impossible to draw a word picture which will convey an adequate impression of their splendour. On either side the trees rise tier above tier, a wealth of foliage abounds everywhere, sweet scents fill the air and the trickling of the river Lemon on one side and the leat on the other is the only sound save the singing of the birds which relieves the prevailing quietitude.'

And back to the Rev. Stirling: 'The sluice by which the leat diverges from the Lemmon at the west corner of the wood offers a resting place where while the ear is delighted with the sinless notes which make the dell vocal, the eye is no less pleased by the gambols of the little fishes as they sport in the liquid stream.' Isn't that delightful?

Mr Bath told me that the ford at Ogwell was more than likely in use

11. The peace of Bradley Meadow.

12. Wishing - or Holy Well.

13. Bradley Manor.

14. It goes in here, and . . .

15. It comes out here.

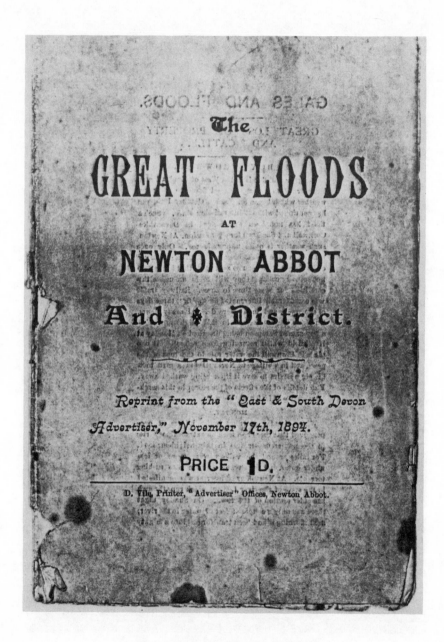

The
GREAT FLOODS
AT
NEWTON ABBOT
And ❧ District.

Reprint from the " East & South Devon

Advertiser," November 17th, 1894.

PRICE 1D.

D. Vile, Printer, "Advertiser" Offices, Newton Abbot.

16. Leaflet of great flood of 1894.

long before 'The Roman came to Rye or out to Severn strode', once more the study of the hedgerows dating them as pre Norman, and the 'relic' meadows either side where he has found pale flax proving the pasture has been undisturbed for centuries and untreated with chemicals. He added that a beautifully polished Neolithic axe probably made of greenstone or volcanic rock from the Knowles hill area had been found in the bed of the river during the last century.

Woods and trees are always exploited by the people of their time, and Bradley is no exception, last being coppiced in 1918 when the alders were cut down and used to make clogs, being shaped and rough hewn on the spot by the men who felled them. But it has also had its moments of history, for the Rev. William Yeo, for fourteen years the clergyman in charge of the parish and church of Wolborough, was the founder of the body from which the Congregational church eventually sprang. He was ejected from Wolborough in 1662 and used to hold meetings at night in the pit on the Ogwell side of the woods. In 1672 he was licensed as a minister and Rhodes goes on to tell us in his History of Newton that he preached in Newton Bushel and in 1689 his house at Rydon was licensed as a place of general worship. He conducted his services in this pit for those who desired liberty to worship God according to the dictates of their conscience and who were compelled to leave the church they loved and find a place for a service of prayer and praise among the quiet beauty of the rock and woods in God's own temple. He resigned his living and to avoid persecution so rife in those troublous times met his sympathising parishioners by night in Bradley woods for the worship of God till a chapel was built in Wolborough Street at which he became minister and thus the founder of Non Conformity in Newton Abbot.

Mr Norman Roberts, a solicitor in Newton Abbot, also a councillor and non conformist, bought the pit with right of access and presented it to the Congregational church, which is now part of the United Reform Cburch. This pit in which they held their meetings two hundred years ago is about thirty feet deep with rocky sides and coarse undergrowth, whilst a fringe of trees entirely hides it until one is almost on its edge. What a place to find in winter! A memorial service is still held annually with fallen trees as benches, those still standing forming some kind of roof with the birds as choir, it really does have the atmosphere of a temple of nature.

The pit itself has various names such as Preacher's Pit, The Devil's Pit -

no doubt by the opposition! - and Gruti's Pit, a very old dialect name for the Devil.

As we near the town we can hear the hum of traffic in the distance, but there are two more interesting things to note in connection with the woods before we leave. Mr J.H. Bibbings, chemist in the town, advertised in an old book his perfume entitled 'Bradley Woods Bouquet' thus . . . 'It will last longer than any other scent - nothing has been spared in its production, the whole world being ransacked for its most precious and costly odours . . . the very souls of flowers pent in walls of glass. After 20 years the unanimous opinion of the public is that it is immeasurably superior to all other bouquets, handkerchiefs sprinkled with it give off whole volumes of enchanting odours and retain the perfume even after repeated washings. Clothes sprinkled with it are proof against the ravages of moths etc., I would point to its immense sale amongst all classes of society. 1/- upwards. Also in sample tubes at 3d and 9d.' Follow that you whizz kids of the television commercial!

Mr Arthur Bibbings, son of J.H. Bibbings, recently retired himself, allowed me to try some of this perfume which he still has and I can only say it is beautiful and lives up to every letter of the advertisement which is more than can be said of most present day advertising.

The second thing of great interest and beauty is, of course, Bradley Manor House where once the river came much nearer to the building, straight across the meadow. Now it has eaten its way across to the other side, and Mrs Woolner, who lives in the house with her family, told me 'Rivers always move like snakes and the bends work downstream, the softness of the ground allowing it to move. In fact higher up the river near horse pool by Ogwell Mill, timber has been put across to try and stop it because it is eating in one side and building up the other.'

This beautiful old manor house dates from the thirteenth century, although it is usually thought of as fifteenth as the east wing was built during that period when the earlier south wing was also remodelled. The east wing is a complete fifteenth century house in itself, a chapel being added at the NE corner in 1428, but the present building begun by the Bushel family in the thirteenth century was not the first house on the site, the earliest buildings most likely being made of wood, and Commander Woolner has made a map of Bradley woods showing near the Manor house, Kiln Orchard, which tells of the potter's art practised there many years ago, and next to it is Culver Orchard so called because there would have stood the manorial Columbarium which was so often built on so lordly a scale as to contain hundreds of doves or pigeons, and beyond lay the Stray Park where wandering animals would be confined.

Mrs Woolner gave the house to the National Trust in 1938, she and her husband and family still living there as tenants of the Trust. The seventy acres of woodland and meadow are free and open to the public at all times, and the house itself can be seen on certain days of the week. She told me, 'There are many stories about the leat, and secret passages; there was meant to be a tunnel running from the hill to Ford House in Newton Abbot where ill starred lovers met, but the truth is it was simply the beginnings of an adit into the hillside, made in an endeavour to start a mine, which I am glad to say didn't materialise! How the tale of the two lovers arose I don't know, unless an unwelcome suitor came up by boat, clandestinely meeting the daughter of the house in the woods. There was one serious incident though during the last century, at election time when feelings ran high, and a policeman who was trying to keep a riotous crowd in order was held face down in the leat till he drowned.'

As well as the river itself, the old mill stream known as the Bradley leat, taken from the river, runs into the town to supply what were the manorial mills. Into this leat by the stone bridge runs a spring from the hill behind, piped into what is called the Wishing Well. The water is still used in the house, never having been known to dry up. The actual leat was probably taken off at the weir during the seventeenth century, coming down to the corner of the field behind the house where it ran underneath controlled by a sluice gate, the rest going on to the town for the mills. Mrs Woolner told me 'this was used for cleaning the stable yeard and probably to carry away the garbage as well!'

The spring water was said to have healing properties, and when Mr Bath was teaching a class of local children he asked them what they knew about the Holy or Wishing Well. One small girl said 'My Mum told me when she was a little girl the lady next door had a baby born blind. She took it to the doctor and he told her to bathe its eyes in water from the spring at Bradley ... she did, and do you know, it could see!'

A story, like the three bears, handed down by mouth from generation to generation, perhaps going back to the Middle Ages. But the truth is the well may have certain healing powers as the chalybeate or natural water contains iron salts which can cure sore eyes. Perhaps to be more prosaic one should add, at one time Pinsent's Brewery in Newton Abbot had pipes bringing the water down to their premises for use in making their beer, and these still run down to what is now White's Garage.

The whole scene must be much the same as it was in the Middle Ages, and there is a strict rule that no vehicles may be brought on the property except when visiting the house. A drive comes down from the main Totnes road to the Lemon Bridge built in 1825 where three parishes meet - Highweek, Wolborough and East Ogwell. From here footpaths go in various directions, across the river by Ghost Bridge up to Ogwell down, over the leat beside the well a path leads into church path and out to the Ashburton Road, then the old public footpath runs beside the leat, passing the house, between the leat and the Lemon through the woods back to Chercombe. But we now take the other by the bridge which leads on to Bradley lane and the town ...

THE URBAN RIVER

Once the river reaches the town its whole character changes. It becomes drab, exploited, rubbish filled, hemmed in by high concrete walls, but at one time, even in its short course through Newton Abbot, it was a very real source of power - an industrious river.

Mr Woolcock, another local historian, said 'I can remember Mr Samson the pork butcher used to wash the sausage skins in a trough at the side of the shop, the water coming from Bradley leat. It's now covered over and was at the side of White's Garage, formerly Pinsent's Brewery, and in old times men used to hand pump water from the leat to cleanse the market.'

It seems until the early 1850s the Lemon was an open river through Market Street from Foss's corner to the Bradley Inn, and a pretty horrible sight and smell it must have been, little more than a cess pit.

Mr Percy Zealley, who has a superb old map of the town dated 1843 told me that even in his day 'In Sun Court, which used to be a cluster of cottages where the reserved car park is now, you had to be careful, if you didn't look out you had all the upstairs slops come on your head! The cottages were on one side and the toilets on the other, but everything went

44

down the street and into the river, and then they used to go to the same source for their drinking water!'

No wonder the Rev. Stirling said in his book "It is said that the disease emphatically called the plague, visited Newton Abbot about the year 1665 and carried off every individual that remained in the town; but I can find no account of this in the chronicles of that time.'

Another Court also stood near Whites, where Mr White, the blacksmith, had a shop behind what is now the baker's shop and the Red Cross Depot. He made wheels for carts, iron ranges, as well as shoeing horses. You can still see the remains of the smithy chimney. Here too Union Bridge crosses the river, joining the ancient parishes of Newton Bushel and Newton Abbot.

In 1836 things improved a little, Royal Assent being given for improving the approach to the town from the Exeter side through Kingsteignton, and Stirling in his History of Newton Abbot tells us that 'The New Market was built in 1826 at an expense of £3000 upwards . . . and the Bradley Inn is as suitable a companion to the new market . . . and possesses every requisite convenience for the accommodation of the public. On passing the tollgate the eye is met by one of those picturesque mills so common in the dells of Devonshire. It is called Serbonemill, now in the occupation of Mr Stockman which stands on the only spot of earth which still retains the ancient name of Newton Abbot. From this point the walk is along the winding banks of the Lemmon to Newton-quay . . .'

I also quote from a letter from Mr Percy Zealley to the Advertiser in which he said 'From records in my possession the Lemon was covered in from the point where it runs under the shop formerly owned by Mr W.T. Harvey in Bank St, then known as Bridge St, and reappeared in the open opposite where Mr H. Michelmore's office now stands. The river remained open from this point until 1903 when it was covered up to Hero's Bridge by the council at a cost of £2,280 by my father the late Mr F.J. Zealley to create the cattle and sheep market now the site of an open car park. Other points of interest are that in 1843 boats were used to bring produce to the Market and a wharf is shown on the map opposite the existing road between the present cattle market and sheep markets. Timber was also floated up to Cull's Timber Yard which was situated on a triangular plot of land between Lloyd's Bank and Sherborne Road, now part of the car park. At this time there were no buildings on the left side of Courtenay Street between the Globe Hotel, then called the Devon Arms, and Hero Bridge. From 1904 onwards development took place in Courtenay Street and around the cattle market and the old market buildings were extended.'

Mr Mudge now lives in a house in Marsh road built by Culls by the side of the river near the old slipway and he remembers the boats coming up from Teignmouth at full tide so the people might shop in the town.

But to return to the work the river had to do, and its first job on reaching the town was at Bradley Mills, the biggest and most prosperous mill of all, run by the Vicary family who were said to have been engaged in the wool and allied trades as long ago as the sixteenth century, the founder of the Newton Bushel wool business being Robert Vicary.

In 1776 his son Moses was born and owing to ill health, in 1786 an Indenture was made between Robert Vicary of Crediton, Fellmonger, and his son Moses of Highweek, Woolcomber, in which the father resigned his business to his son on condition he pay his father two shillings a week! There is a family legend that his mother Elizabeth came by horseback to Newton Bushel with her little son and carried on the business until he was of age to fend for himself, and this is correct. She died at the age of eighty-nine in 1843, but to Moses and his father in law, Gilbert Doke, much of the credit of the industrial development of Newton Abbot is due, and their success in turn to the River Lemon which ran their mills.

They extended from woolcombing, wool dealing and fellmongering to tanning. Unfortunately there is no space here to develop the story of this remarkable family, which would make a saga in itself, but it must just be said that in spite of numerous set backs and difficulties, through the Napoleonic wars, the industrial stress of 1821 and the Hungry Forties, they stuck it out, and from the *Mid Devon Advertiser* of May 1952 I quote: 'The mills are increasing their production - reconstruction is being carried out up to half a million pounds to treble the factory's output and double the employees. The tanning industry founded by the Vicary family at Bradley about 150 years ago, noted throughout the world for the quality of leather produced, also fellmongering, the stripping and combing of wool from the hides. Now the tanning of leather has been displaced by this and the building reconstructed to house the best of modern wool combing machinery, sent to spinners all over the world.

'Round the clock work goes on at Bradley, the largest combing factory in South England. Five hundred bales of greasy wool clipped from the backs of sheep in Australia and S. Africa are processed each week, a machine called a "willey" knocks out the solid matter and this is collected in sacks and sold as shoddy manure, a top dressing for agriculture, this includes sand, mud and bits of plants . . . '

All of which was confirmed by Mr Billings of Highweek who used to help wash this wool and said the mud was put on the ground at the back of the mill where all kinds of peculiar plants grew, including eucalyptus and burrs of enormous size!

But more mills took their livelihood from the river. One of these belonged originally to Bradley Manor and Mrs Woolner told me in those days it was called Shirburne, the name being very old coming originally from the words Shire Burn, a clear or boundary stream, possibly making the mill older even than the Manor itself. In those days the mill stood low in the river in Mill Lane, now Halycon Road. You can still follow the leat most of the way, although it is covered over now behind the South Devon Cricket Club ground, which stands between it and the river, and here again we are in the midst of history, for over 150 years ago a cricket club was formerly established at Teignbridge, although the game had actually been played in Devon during 1823, and perhaps rather surprisingly, Parson Jack Russell who is normally associated with terriers and hunting, was one of the members who met in a barn at this time. It seems from the records of the meeting that it was a s difficult then as it is now to find a large enough flat field in the local countryside to accommodate a full sized pitch!

Sadly now all the mills are hushed in the town as in the country, silenced by progress, by the growth of synthetics, and by the cheap imports, a bitter blow to the industry of the town, but nothing stops our river running on. Recently I walked along its bed through the tunnel where it runs under the town, guided by two men from the Council Engineering dept, Peter Daymon and Ken White, their job being to keep it clear of obstruction.

It was an eerie feeling as trout swim round your feet while soft stalactites hanging from the concrete roof brush your face. We went in just beyond Union Bridge looking up many feet above our heads at the plaque let into the wall recalling the height of the devastating floods of 1938. Soon we walked into darkness below the shops in Bank Street, past huge metal storm doors which line the side and open automatically when the pressure builds up behind them. For some obscure reason most of the rubbish here seemed to consist of old exhaust pipes from motor cars!

There is complete silence except for the swish of the river. Traffic noise is non-existent, all we could hear was the pounding of the automatic drills above us where the road was being repaired. It was quite a relief to come out into the daylight by Hero Bridge, near the bus station. Here at one time stood Marlborough House, standing within a stone's throw of the market and yet with spacious grounds. It was built in 1842, one of the first houses on the newly cut road from Newton to Kingsteignton mentioned earlier. Daniel Vile bought it in 1902. Founder and editor of the *Advertiser* in 1863, his life is a real rags to riches story, for he had been born in Crediton in 1838 and worked as a farm labourer, but he attended night school and eventually worked for a firm of printers, publishing a sheet called the *Newton Journal*. When it went broke Daniel was offered the business and worthless machinery in lieu of wages. In 1863 he published the first issue of the *East and South Devon Advertiser*. It paid and eventually he sold out at a price which assured him of a comfortable retirement, which he spent at Marlborough House until he died in 1915.

But although our river was industrious, it was also mischievous and took its toll of human life, numerous children being swept away as well as cattle. For many years a memorial notice appeared in the local paper for a small boy drowned in 1948 at the age of three whose body was never recovered, and Freda Wilkins of Poundsgate told me of a child who fell in the river when it was in spate and thick with mud. At Hero Bridge a soldier dived in to rescue it, a stranger who did not realise the water was only a couple of feet deep above the paved bottom, and although the child was saved, the man was severely injured.

Drowning was not all the trouble it caused for finally come the stories of the floods which have hit the town and surrounding countryside.

STORM AND TEMPEST

The first actual account I could find of serious flooding in the town was in 1853, although of course ever since there was any kind of settlement in the area, the floods must have been extensive. This account is as follows: 'A flood occurred of a nature most detrimental to health and property on the evening of 19th December as a result of which after much arguing and

17. In Memory of a Flood.

18. 1938 Flood scenes in Newton Abbot.

19. 1938 Flood scenes in Newton Abbot.

20. Taking the plunge.

21. Car or boat?

22. Come to the races and bring your seahorse.

▲ 23. A future pioneer? Theron Melland braves the
flood waters of 1974.

▼ 24. Marsh Road. February 1974.

25. A River's Swan Song.

many meetings the way the wardens of the parish of Wolborough lowered the bed of the Lemon under the county arch two feet and also lowered the bed throughout its course from the Union Bridge formerly called the Way behind the Forded Wooden Bridge to another point further down . . . the damage done by the flood in the lower parts of this and the adjoining borough must have been to a great extent caused by encroachment made from time to time by persons possessing property on either side of the river Lemon as well as on either side of the drain anciently called Tuckings Leat or river which runs at the back of Market Terrace and the Mill Leat . . . we present that the stewards and officers of the court should on any occasion of building or alteration being carried on adjoining the Lemon induce the owner or other person concerned to give up to the water course as much land as might possibly be spared . . . ' but I was fortunate enough to be given two separate accounts of the floods of 1894, one from Mrs Stoneman of Halycon Road who is ninety and remembers these very well, the other from Mr T.M. Holwill of Southernhay in Newton Abbot. In each case the headings were horrendous - as the floods themselves must have been, and the best way I can convey this is by giving some extracts from these leaflets.

THE EAST AND SOUTH DEVON ADVERTISER OF
NOVEMBER 17th 1894 price 1d.

'Gales and floods - Great Loss of Property and Cattle -
Boy drowned.

'The gales and floods in the west of England may be regarded as a sort of grand finale to the rainy weather which began on Friday October 19th and continued without intermission since - at Newton such weather is quite unprecedented and in many cases houses have become so saturated that if they do not actually collapse they will be in an unhealthy condition for some time to come . . . great interest was manifested in the state of the river Lemon which runs through the older portion of the town - on Sunday there was only a couple of feet of water in the river - next morning it had been transformed into a mighty torrent the colour of pea soup, rushing along at the rate of 10 or 12 miles an hour. Business in the town was almost entirely suspended and the public thoroughfare deserted. No London trains arrived after 9 a.m. from Paddington . . . some lads circulated an entirely unfounded report to the effect that two children had been drowned in Bradley Meadow . . on Tuesday the Lemon was higher than on Monday . . water got into a large number of houses and a boat was requisitioned for the convenience of the inhabitants . . . men were engaged in pumping out water at the Gas Works all day and night . . . Wednesday is a day which will be remembered in Newton for years to come (on only one previous occasion can even the oldest inhabitants remember when the Lemon caused so much mischief - a flood of similar nature occurred on December 16th 1853 - 41 years ago - boats then plying in what is now Courtenay St and Bank St. Since then the river bed has been deepened and a sewer built.) The water rushed down until between 9 and 10, it overflowed into White's Lane and poured into Sun Court - by 12 it was running out of the windows on the ground floor and people had to abandon their houses. Tradesmen in Wolborough St had to remove their horses, the water rising two feet in 15 minutes . . . groceries were destroyed including 5 tons of soda. Mr Gibbons who occupied part of the premises for 25 years never knew such a thing to occur before . . . at the back of Messrs Mill's brewery were 11 pigs, colts and horses. By the time they had been removed the horses were only just able to keep their feet . . . meanwhile things were particularly interesting in Bank and Market Streets . . . like a new river flooding the shops. The efforts put forward to stop the flood were as practicable as the efforts of the celebrated Mrs Partington to keep back the sea with a broom. No access could be gained to the post office, temporary platforms were made with planks and ladders to enable persons to go in and out, and banks of clay put in front of the doors. In the dressing rooms of Alexandra Hall were five feet of water. Trout were picked up in a garden at the back of Linden Terrace . . . early in the afternoon an elderly mare which had been grazing in a field adjoining the turnpike in Totnes road got over the hedge, it wandered down Palk's Court in Wolborough St. Here the Lemon had overflowed and the animal got in the river. It was carried under the tunnel into Market St, emerging to sight near the market. The water having reached the tops of the arches of the bridge the animal was bumped against the stonework, an attempt being made to pull it ashore at Lemon Road. One man did actually catch hold of its mane but the force of the current carried it away again. Lower down near the bridge in Lemon road another, and this time successful, attempt was made to save the animal by means of

58

ropes. The horse lay on the ground in an exhausted state for some time after, and was eventually taken to the stables of Mr A.R. Williams, Veterinary surgeon, who applied restoratives. A severe cut in the animal's forehead was sewn up by Mr Williams. A great quantity of water entered the animal's lungs setting up inflammation and it is still in a critical condition. The marvel is that it should have survived at all after being washed along for half a mile in a roaring torrent, for nearly quarter the distance, under water . . . in the marsh district behind Lower St Paul's road was a lake in which some boys amused themselves by paddling about in boats and on rafts - a salmon was jumping about in the water in the marshes on Wednesday.

'It is very questionable if there have been similar heavy floods during the present century - it is true that about the middle of December 1853 Newton was the scene of extraordinary floods, so high did the Lemon on that occasion overflow its bank that a hay rick in Bradley meadows, where a portion of Vicary's tanyard is now, was bodity carried away by the stream and washed through White's Lane and finally lodged against a building used for the sale of fish near where the Alexandra Hall now stands . . . Mr Roberts remembers it well, but is of the opinion the former was not nearly as great as the latter. The Lemon had not such a free let out then as now. Well this is so otherwise the consequences, great as they were on Wednesday last, would without doubt have been more lamentable.

'Wednesday morning ushered in with torrents of rain, rain, rain, nothing but rain. Everyone was feeling angry with the elements and the more angry people got the more their feelings were reflected in the thick and dark overcast . . . the river rushing on in its apparent mad career towards the sea, its water red with rage . . . however Mr W. Dunn who always delights in solving knotty problems and investigating everything of local interest was even equal to this occasion for without divesting himself of any of his clothes he waded through stream after stream with boyish glee the water causing his watch to stop. Even the mighty stream in White's lane deterred him not. He struggled on with a majestic tread and a face full of smiles against the current in this thoroughfare until reaching the bottom of Sun Court where he encountered a treacherous pit occasioned by the floods which nearly took him off his feet . . . Mr Dunn has indelibly associated his name with the great floods of 1894 . . . '

These next extracts are from a leaflet written by Mr Chandler of the

Western Morning News.

'Wednesday last November 14th will long be memorable in Newton Abbot for on that day for the first time for more than 40 years the town was flooded by the overflowing of the river Lemon . . . usually the Lemon is an insignificant little stream but owing to very heavy rains which have fallen almost without a break for three weeks past it has lately been swollen much above its average height. Mr Calvertt, draper, was badly attacked behind by the waters, the walls of his shop forming the left bank of the river as it enters the long tunnel under Market St. The water lept up the wall 15 feet or more, a roaring furious whirlpool, grand and yet awful to witness, the brown waters dashing madly on their headlong course foamed and roared with deafening loudness. They reached the window of the carpet room 18 feet above the level of the water . . . the local Board men commenced operations to raise a dam below his premises which would have the effect of ponding back the water and completely drenching his place . . . he remonstrated and pointed out what the result would be . . . the men however had orders and proceeded to carry them out regardless of anybody . . . Mr Calvertt began kicking the dam away . . . this drew a crowd . . . Englishmen always applaud the weaker side and Mr Calvertt being one against a number of brawny workmen, and having feet only against their shovels, received the lions share of the applause . . . eventually he came off the victor . . .

'Ladies were imprisoned in shops . . . some raised their skirts and waded through the water rewarded by rounds of laughter . . . nowhere was the flood worse than in Sun Court and remembering that all the people affected there are poor cottagers, residing where rent is cheapest, it is more than sad to think of the damage done to the furniture . . . in the afternoon I attempted to explore the Court . . . it is a miserably dark approach and every step I took in the nasty coloured liquid I asked myself if the place was called Sun Court because the sun really does shine there sometimes . . . Mrs Noyce who lived there told me she hadn't been warm since Wednesday . . . she has lived in Newton 70 years and well remembers the flood of 43 years ago. That was much worse than the late flood she said . . . I went into Mrs Aggett's in Victoria place . . . the front room was in confusion . . . at the far end of a very dark room was a decrepit looking old man doing his little best. Mrs Aggett said "I could not clean it up, the water overpowers me. Poor old soul, he is doing his best, he ought not to be there, he's been ill for

15 years and this will not do him any good." I thought so too . . . '

I liked Mr Chapman's tail piece . . . 'The foregoing account of the floods is by no means complete. It has been written in a few hours at the request of Mr S. Wotton the publisher and having other important matters on hand at the same time I have been unable to devote as much attention to it as the subject demanded.'

I know just how he felt.

Now from the *Mid Devon Advertiser* of Saturday 6th August 1938 I give extracts of the floods of that period in contrast to the others . . . 'MID DEVON SWEPT BY THE WORST STORMS IN LIVING MEMORY . . . RAGING TORRENT LEAVES HAVOC IN ITS WAKE. Newton Abbot was hit by the worst storms in the district ever experienced . . . trains held up, premises flooded, animals killed, houses struck by lightning, people marooned, cars abandoned . . . On Wednesday night masses of clouds gathered in the west and the air was still, hot and oppressive seemingly charged with electricity. The dawn streaked sky was suffused with a pink and orange eerie glow and split by continuous forked lightning. The rain fell not like an English storm but with tropical malevolence and appeared to threaten destruction to the world beneath . . . in the brilliant flashes of lightning objects stood out clearly . . . pathetic stories of damage could be heard on every hand . . . lights began to appear in downstairs windows showing people had been drawn from the comfort of their beds and the terrified barking of dogs could be heard. The river Lemon which had been rushing along its bed for some hours like a raging torrent was unrecognisable compared with the placid summer stream . . . defences were hurriedly constructed and people dashed about with boards, sacks and all manner of barriers which were being erected in an effort to stem the flood . . . but the raging torrent was not to be denied . . . many people donned bathing costumes, football shorts and waders in their efforts, fetching milk and other necessities . . . few motorists dared drive through the streets . . . never before had flooding on such an extensive scale occurred in Newton Abbot . . . Mrs Preston had to be rescued from her bedroom in Back Lane by means of a ladder, a number of sheep in Bradley Meadow were driven to safety but two ponies at the back of the Golden Lion Inn were drowned . . . the staff of the Odeon Cinema had to cope with water four feet deep in the car park and by a remarkable coincidence the film being shown was 'The Hurricane"! doubtless the staff were gaining first hand knowledge of such a storm. Seale Hayne Met. station reported 4.35 inches of rain fell from 5 a.m. to 10 a.m. and .5 from 10 to 3 p.m. a total of nearly 5 inches in 10 hours . . . the main streets resembled canals . . . at Bickington the river Lemon overflowed early on Thursday morning, a haystack by the bank covered to within a couple of feet of the top, water washed produce out of low lying ground sweeping chicken houses in its path. The bridge at New Cross was totally destroyed cutting off the easiest entrance to the village, the bowling green pavilion and equipment were swept away and at Owen Caunter's house, Bonemill, buildings were flooded, his living quarters suffering the worst damage, and the little humped bridge over the river close by destroyed leaving oddly enough one of the arches as the sole remains over which Owen proceeded to walk. Just after 7 o'clock the fire brigade had to discharge two maroons to summon men, and one of them said "It was just like having the Victoria falls, a howitzer battery and a searchlight tattoo in one's own back garden . . ." The river which had been a mere trickle in its bed the night before, by morning was a raging torrent. It burst through in the same places again - Clarendon and Grafton roads making holes of 25 to 30 ft wide through very substantial masonry - it went through as if made of paper, there was a tremendous rush of water between the backs of the roads which brought terror to the inhabitants, women screaming as they rushed their children to safety . . . a garden at the back of the house occupied by Mr and Mrs Blackler in Clarendon Road appeared to have been struck by an h.e. shell . . . Vicary's mill was flooded, Reids Garage, Western Garage - the river swept on down Back Street and both Courtenay Street and Queen Street experienced miniature tidal waves . . . at Devon Square the water turned off by the Imperial Theatre into Lemon road . . . as usual there was a lighter side - the staff of Devon General Omnibus Co., put a five foot tall tomato plant in the market square when the floods subsided, giving the semblance that it had sprung up as a result of the copious watering . . . '

Mr Arthur Bibbings who took the old photographs of the floods told me 'The owner of the submerged car in Bank St had been in the post office, he came out and just stood watching, unable to believe his eyes . . . but not only did the river overflow, but the sewers too and the boy apprentice and I who had been in the water up to our armpits to take photos, stank like a midden!'

Mr Mudge of Marsh road showed me the second account in the

Advertiser of the last flooding of the town in February 1974 . . . somehow it all sounds familiar . . . 'When the river Lemon flooded the lower part of the town the urban councillors had to postpone normal business to demand a report on the situation from Mr Barry Mole, the surveyor, when they were told the bulk of the water from the moor had not yet reached the town . . . there had been the highest tide for 300 years with gale force winds and 10 inches of rain falling in the town in January and February . . . some residents accused the NARDC for not being prepared for the floods, but the deputy surveyor Mr Batten said "We had six men filling sandbags on Friday . . . the tides and rain were exceptional, you can't foretell these things . . .a lot of time and money would be needed to prevent the volume of flooding of this type again . . ." '

And so we come to the end of our journey and the life story of the river. Sadly, as it runs under the dark iron railway bridge to join the Teign, it is sleazy still, hemmed in by concrete, surrounded by demolished factories and works, filled with old junk and sluggish with oil . . . like a human being, its life started with promise, with freshness and innocence and beauty. Living has scarred it and now it looks weary and glad to relinquish its work. At least there is a sweet smelling weed with white blossom covering the banks and a family of swans preen themselves among the slimy stones so perhaps it would be kinder just to call this its swan song.

THE 1979 FLOOD DISASTER

When, in the last chapter, I wrote of storm, tempest and floods in Newton Abbot along the banks of the Lemon, I gave an extract from the *Mid Devon Advertiser* of 6 August 1938 in which it said: 'WORST STORMS IN LIVING MEMORY. RAGING TORRENT LEAVES HAVOC IN ITS WAKE. Newton Abbot was hit by the worst storms in the district ever experienced.' I had no idea that it would only be a few months after I had written those words that the very same could - and would - be said. The issue of the same newspaper dated 29 December 1979 has as its heading, 'DELUGE OF DISASTER. Area hit by the worst floods for 40 years.'

In 1853 an old account told of 'a flood of a nature most detrimental to health and property on the evening of 19th Dec.' If you read any of the accounts of the numerous floods, allowing for a slightly altered style of actual reporting, most of them could be speaking of this last occasion.

We, ourselves, watched the river rise rapidly all day until we were surrounded by torrents of thick yellow water. Every half hour we went into the garden with a torch to see how it was creeping towards the house. We took valuable files of papers, etc., upstairs. Then suddenly about 10 p.m., just as if someone had pulled out the bath plug, it started to go down. It was nothing to do with the tide which wasn't full till after midnight - no, this was when the poor souls in Newton Abbot had a giant wave about five feet high sweep through the town. Stone walls along the backs of the houses in the cul de sacs that lead off Wolborough Street felt the impact as it rushed on down and into the main streets of the town, swirling into shops, pubs and hotels, sometimes nearly five feet high or more.

My friend Owen Caunter at Bone Mill Farm had also carried most of his possessions upstairs for the water had started to come up through his floorboards and he well remembered the devastation of 1938. However, next day when I saw him he told me it had gone down before it actually did any damage.

But we were two of the lucky ones. I went into town on Friday morning - it could only be described as a disaster area. In fact Andrew Cooper, the well-known local artist and natural historian, told me he had been in the town during the night hours and the only word he could use for it was 'hairy'. It really was a terrifying nightmare,' he said. 'Little boats were being tossed about and the police and marines were trying to persuade people to come out of their flats and homes because of the danger from electricity apart from the water itself.'

Next morning people were trying to brush out the filth from their business premises and homes. The streets were piled high with every conceivable type of merchandise: beautiful luxury books, books with priceless coloured illustrations, piles of paperbacks, carpets, furniture, shoes, clothes, fridges - you name it and there it stood - ruined. To add to the horror and discomfort all the electricity had been turned off because of flooding in the sub stations so all work had to be done by the light of candles with no heating. Even on the following Wednesday many town centre shops and homes still had no electricity.

But it is really the people who live in the small houses and villas in the side streets who suffered the most with their piles of pathetic belongings outside their homes - bedraggled Christmas trees, broken toys, soaking chairs and carpets - and it is inevitable once more to compare past and present. Clarendon and Grafton Road as well as Linden Terrace and Waltham Road suffered terrible damage, huge holes of 25-30 feet being made in the retaining walls. Elsewhere I have told the story of 1938 and Mr and Mrs Blackler in Clarendon Road who had a huge wave sweep through their house and garden as if a high explosive bomb had hit it.

This time it was the turn of Marjorie and Joe Luscombe who live at 13 Clarendon Road, next to the river. It left a trail four feet high through the house. They were having dinner and at the time Mrs Luscombe said the conditions didn't seem too bad, but later she went upstairs to look from the bedroom window and saw it had reached the top of the bank. She went back downstairs and opened the back door and a torrent of water rushed in. Like most people in similar circumstances, they were extremely reluctant to leave their home but were eventually persuaded by firemen who carried them off to the Rescue Centre. At 10 o'clock on Friday morning they went back to find a devastated house - but Marjorie was determined to clear up the mess and stay put. She said, 'It is the second time in less than five years we have been flooded, but we have been here for 23 years, it is our home - and there is nothing we can do about it.'

26. 5.25 p.m. Thursday 27 December 1979. St. Leonards Tower from the Wolborough Street side looking towards Courtenay Street.
(Mid Devon Advertiser)

I went to talk to Sheila and Neville Tortoiseshell who live in what used to be Ogwell Mill, a picture of which is shown as No. 8 in this book. They have been there six months rebuilding the bungalow which replaced the original mill. Whilst this work was being done they lived in the orchard in a caravan, and had moved into the house a week before the floods. 'A good thing we did,' Sheila told me, 'for nearly a foot of water swept through the caravan.' Her new kitchen units had just been delivered and screwed down to the floor when the water started to rise. 'Had it not been for our marvellous friends in Ogwell Village, the water would have flooded through the house. They came with plastic sacks, laundry bags and pedal bin liners, they filled them with sand the builders had left, and piled them along the garden hedge. They worked like slaves and certainly saved us.' She showed me the tide mark on the wall. 'Some other kind souls had already taken the two children back to the village with them for safety, and then just before midnight I looked out and suddenly the water receded a little, so at last we could go to bed.'

Frederick Martin, general manager of the *Western Times* in Exeter, who lives at Doddiscombeleigh, had his own news story which nearly ended in tragedy. His car was swept away in the swollen waters of the Teign as he drove along the B3193 and turned off for home at the Teign House Inn, Christow. The flood water swept his car 100 yards off the road, but he managed to get out and wade to the inn.

Apart from shops in the town, of course, there are many other industries, one of the best known being Edwin Tucker's Maltings. Richard Wheeler, one of the directors, told me: 'On Thursday midday I could see the flood water building up. I got hold of our electrician but there was already about five feet of water in the building. There was nothing we could do - the tide came up so quickly we just had to stand and watch the electric motors being engulfed. The corn is in the growing process at the moment, and we managed to shovel most of that up on the kilns, but all our heating and drying had gone. heaven knows what the damage will be.' He told me the Sports Centre, too, had been devastated with all the floors, squash courts and tennis courts broken up by flood water.

Val Mason cuts my hair for me - a lively, happy young girl, until their home at 22 Grafton Road was ruined by flood water on Thursday. 'It started just before lunch; we rang the council but they told us it wouldn't come any higher.' By 9 o'clock that night it had swept over the walls and

▲ 27. Left - River Lemon; Right - Marsh Road by gasometer.
▼ 28. Corner of Bank St. and Wolborough St., Thursday evening.
(Mid Devon Advertiser)

swirled into No. 22 at least four feet deep. 'It came up through the bath, the sink and the loo. As fast as we baled it out of the bathroom it came back through the kitchen. We took what we could upstairs, but they are too narrow for furniture and our chairs and sofa are ruined. Fortunately the telly we'd bought for Christmas we managed to save, but when Mum and I came down on Friday morning we just didn't know where to start. There were sausages floating around the kitchen, the units and cooker were full of filthy stinking mud, we couldn't find any saucepans or china . . . at the moment we have to sit in deck chairs on a soaking wet floor, watching the telly.' She managed to smile. 'At least we do have a fire . . . ' As usual the spirit of the people was fantastic. Someone said to me: 'Just like the war, only this time the little groups of people are talking of our flood instead of our bomb.'

Special Constable, Jeff Fry, was out with his companion when they

29. Bank Street in flood
(Mid Devon Advertiser)

were called to some cottages where a woman and three children were stranded. They left the car outside with its blue revolving signal light while they fetched the children wrapped in blankets. As they came out of the front door, far away down the road they could just see the blue light flashing - the car had floated 'downstream'. However, they managed to recover it and complete the rescue operations.

It would be impossible to recount anything like all the tragic - and humorous - stories, and it will perhaps be months before the final assessment emerges. People who have gone abroad for a holiday will come back to ruined furniture, and wrangling for money will go on perhaps for years over cause, effect and cure. But none of us who lived through this flood will ever forget it. As I walked the next day along the banks of the swollen river I went to look for the plaque on the wall at the back of the carpark near Union Bridge where the height of the 1938 flood had been commemorated. To my consternation I found it had gone. Fortunately there is a photograph of it I had taken as you can see on Page 49. When I asked the carpark attendant what had happened he told me the demolition contractors had simply knocked down the wall . . . so our picture of this landmark may be unique. Union Bridge itself, built in 1822, only has a breach in the parapet, the rest still stands.

Altogether over a hundred people were evacuated from their homes to the Rescue Centre set up at Coombeshead School in Highweek, and here blankets and hot food were, as always in emergencies, provided by those marvellous people from all the voluntary services. Volunteers, too, filled sandbags until the sand ran out and with quarries closed for the holidays no more could be obtained.

There were small, poignant incidents, like the young farmer who drove his land rover to the station to take back relatives who had been visiting from Exeter. There he found about fifteen people who had arrived at the station and had no means of reaching their homes at such places as Abbotskerswell and Kingsteignton - no buses, no taxis. They were so desperate that some of them were in tears. 'I took all I could,' he said, 'but I was running short of fuel.' The bus station had to be evacuated as a crack appeared in the wall by the river, and all the buses were taken to Torquay, the building itself being under three feet of water. Outside Hullands Bookshop stood a lorry being loaded with the pulpy remains of books, carpets, furniture - one poor assistant looked at me with despair in her eye

30. Osborne Park and carpark *(Mid Devon Advertiser)*

pointing at a pile of paperbaks. 'They include copies of your *Along the Lemon*,' she said bleakly!

In the town Library, where they had just completed the reorganisation of the non-fiction room with a new carpet and shelves, again the water had swept through and to add to their troubles they had no heating as the boiler in the next door building had been put out of action. The three million pound shopping complex opened in May in the centre of town was a shambles of mud, dirty clothes, food, magazines and every kind of rubbish.

At the height of the flood, Courtenay Street, Bank Street and Highweek Street all became rushing torrents and the eight coastguards from Teignmouth and the Royal Marines from Lympstone had difficulty in controlling their boats, one being swept through Oliver's window. All the phones were out of action and the police and AA turned people away from roads leading into the town. The coastguards under John Hook brought

31. Recreation Ground pitches, December 28 *(Mid Devon Adertiser)*

two large rowing boats on a lorry with them and rescued dozens of trapped householders. They stayed in the town for six hours and Mr Hook said he had never seen anything like it. 'Water was ripping through the streets and rescue was made all the more difficult by submerged cars and other objects . . . it looked like a disaster area and the damage must be colossal.' The damage . . . recriminations . . . the hindsight. All these are recorded in the local press:

'Council divers Brian Wright and Terry Morris have been inspecting the bridges which took an enormous pounding when this normally gentle river rose 6 feet in a few hours . . . '

'Mr Les Pike, Teignbridge Council Chairman, toured the worst hit areas and ordered staff to give priority to flood clearance work . . . he has asked for £15,000 to be allocated by the policy committee for emergency work.'

'One food store alone lost £40,000 worth of goods, a furniture store

32. Market Walk pedestrian precinct. *(Mid Devon Advertiser)*

£50,000 . . . commercial premises will have to look after themselves . . . all the effort is being concentrated in helping those whose homes have been flooded.'

'Once the immediate problems are overcome Teignbridge is to press the South West Water Authority to take over full responsibility for the River Lemon.'

'Through no fault of its own Devon County Council faces a huge bill for the cost of the damage caused by floods. Government aid is limited on the basis of a 75% grant of expenditure but only after the produce of a penny rate has been spent . . . ratepayers will have to cough up £1.6 million before any support is available.'

'Newton Abbot was not adequately prepared for the flood havoc which hit the market town this week.' This last comment came from Mrs Nancy Morrison, Mayor of Newton Abbot, and she is to make an official complaint at the next meeting of Teignbridge Council criticising their handling of the disaster. She added that no sandbags and no blankets were available. 'I talked to people myself who had rung up the council for sandbags when they saw the height of the river and were told "No way - the river won't rise any more anyway." That was just after lunch on Thursday.'

Haven't we heard it all before? In February 1974? Look on Page 63 of this book.

Many people who bought the first editions of *Along the Lemon* said they had no idea the River Lemon was such a big river until they read the book - maybe the Council should have given it a close study! Mr Pike, after walking the banks, said he had no idea it was a main river! Now he has no doubt and thinks it should be the responsibility of the South West Water Authority.

One more point must be brought up - new housing estates in the area. There is already a huge complex at Bradley Barton and isn't it odd that since that was built with its drains and sewers the floods are worse than ever? A new estate has been suggested for Ogwell. Mr Usher, who is chairman of the committee set up to fight this new threat, said, 'We are very worried about the extra water flow bound to be created by this new development. The council has decided to build a dam which will hold flood water, but if that overflows it will mean serious problems for Newton Abbot. The River Lemon cannot hold any more water. It will be tragic.'

Mr Reg Willis, a member of the planning committee, has been against these

▲ 33. The market stalls have been replaced by waves.
　▼ 34. Sherborne Road with multi-storey car park in the background.
(Mid Devon Advertiser)

plans from the start. He said, 'If the Ogwell Development is built, Newton Abbot will be in six feet of water. Housing developments in other areas have now put the river at its limits.' He never spoke a truer word and like everyone else who stood watching helplessly as the flood water approached us I say - River, please stay away from my door.

I don't think there could be any more apt ending to such a chapter as extracts from a letter Margery and Joe Luscombe wtote to the *Mid Devon Advertiser* the week after the flood. 'It was another frightening experience at poor old 13 Clarendon Road, Newton Abbot on Thursday last week . . . but how much my husband and I would like to thank everybody who helped. The firemen, Wolborough Scouts Hall, St. Leonard's Church and Coombeshead School who sheltered us for the night, all the wonderful people who worked more than 24 hours looking after us. The man who drove us from Wolborough Street to Coombeshead, the Marines who rushed beds down to us . . . Mr Roger Smith of the Lions' Club, Mrs Christine Sorenson from Social Services, and another lady and gent who helped clear up inches of brown river slime. My husband could not help as he is under medication with heart trouble. A special thank you to our neighbour Brian who every day saw to our heaters, kindly lent by the council to dry out our wet furniture. Then to the electricity and gas people for being so prompt and mending our fuses and to Mr Frank Critchley who was kindness itself. Finally to a lady who drove about seven miles to let my aged parents know we were alright. We sometimes take things for granted but at a time like this when you have had three feet of water through your house - the second disaster in five years - it makes you feel proud to know that there are men and women who will help at any hour, day or night. Finally I would like to ask: will those planners still go ahead at Canada Hill now after this terrible warning?

Margery and Joe Luscombe, 13 Clarendon Road, Newton Abbot.'
That says it all.

I AM A RIVER -
IT WASN'T MY FAULT

I look after about fifty square miles of land between say Newton Abbot and Haytor then back around Denbury to Newton Abbot. My job is to see that it is well drained. But I don't want another job like I had on 27 December 1979. I had no less than 278,780,000 gallons of water to deal with from less than 24 hours' rain.

Well, I started off at Haytor Quarries which is the beginning of my territory, and I was soon rattling along through Pinchaford and then down to Sigford. Here I met gallons of my other friends; they seemed to come from all directions - Bagtor, Halshanger, Owlacombe. I think we got under the bridge alright without causing any damage, but I don't know what happened after I left.

After Sigford I made for Bickington, rattling down this valley at the amazing speed of 4 mph. I didn't expect any problems at Bickington as new wide bridges had recently been built when they made the new road, but I was getting bigger, and there wasn't room the way I usually go. I had to get out over the banks into the fields - much easier going there - as I was being pushed from behind all the time. I would soon be at the bridge at the Dartmoor Halfway. This shouldn't be any problem as a bigger bridge was built here after I washed the old one away back in 1938. Passing Halfway I thought Barry, the landlord, was lucky to be up high and dry as I would have made a mess of his lovely dining rooms and his beautiful carpets.

My next problem was Chipley Bridge. This one I also washed away in 1938, but a bigger one was built soon after. Now Owen Caunter lives here. I didn't want to upset him like I did in 1938 when I swept through his house and spoilt all his furniture, but I was already running all over his fields and also Freddie Westcott's the other side. Now can I get under this bridge or not? I was right up to the very top but I got through without going through Owen's house, but I swamped his garden and went right up to his back door.

Having got through there all right I was on my way to the next bridge, the two at Milltroughs. No problem here. Then on to old Mill at Ingsdon where Chappie Yeo lives - I hope you'd picked up your carpets, Chappie, as I'm not sure I passed you. Now my next problem was Morley Bridge where Judy Chard lives, but before that I have somebody else join me - the Kesterbrook. I said I haven't any room for you - I'm full up already - but I suppose I must take you along. Now down to Judy and Morley Bridge.

There she is watching me coming down past her garden - Hi Judy! I'll try not to do any damage as you've got a lovely little bridge here. Perhaps I can bypass it. Yes, I can, I'll go through this farmer's gateway and cross the road. Oh dear, I've made an awful mess of the road, scoured out a gutter about three feet deep, but it's better than washing your bridge away, isn't it? I must rush on now to Chercombe Bridge passing Commander Holdsworth's Holbeam Mill. I'm sorry Commander if I've caused you any

In the aftermath: one of the places where the Lemon wall was breached

damage but I expect you were well prepared. Ah, Chercombe Bridge. Oh dear, I'm flowing out all over Lionel Stanbury's field - sorry about that Lionel. There's too much of me to get through this bridge, I'll have to cross the road . . . Oh, no, not in that house! Yes . . . I'm sorry, I see I've made an awful mess.

Now down through Bradley Woods into Newton Abbot. I can't do much damage through the woods. Well, here I am at Bradley Mill. Oh dear, there isn't half enough room here, I will have to spill over and find a way down Wolborough Street. Perhaps now I can try to get through my usual way, through the culvert at the back of Mr Smith's baker's shop.

But I can see it is hopeless. It is like trying to get eight inches of water through a four inch pipe. I have to go somewhere as I am being pushed from behind all the time. I know, I'll go through Jim Heath's yard and through his shop into Highweek Street. Sorry about that Jim but it was my quickest way into Highweek Street. Where can I go now? Down into Bank Street and then along the lane past the old Post Office and out by the drum clock. But my goodness! What's this? Buildings right across my path blocking my way. Whoever did this? What a silly thing to do. Where can I go now? Oh yes, there's a small hopway here - I'll try this way. What? Into a big square yard with shops all around. What can I do. I'm trapped. I'll try this carpet shop. Perhaps I can go through and out the back door. What! Trapped again. I'll try this clothes shop . . . no good. I'll try them all . . . dozens of them . . . but no good. I've made an awful mess. I'm sorry you shopkeepers. It's not my fault. I think you must blame the planners of this new market. I must go through Newton Abbot, there's no other way for me. I'm supposed to go through the culvert at the back of Mr Smith's baker's shop, but it's twelve feet wide and eight feet high and will only take part of me - 12,441,600 gallons per hour - but I'm coming into Newton Abbot at 28,472,880 gallons per hour today. What I think you should have done was to build a bigger culvert for me before you built this new market. You had a golden opportunity then, but you'll have to do something before I come down in flood again. Maybe this year . . . maybe next . . . maybe not for fifty years . . . but I'm sure to be back.

Sorry folks . . . don't blame me.

Signed RIVER LEMON
(Owen Caunter)

OTHER BOOKS
from
ORCHARD PUBLICATIONS